STARS OF SPORTS

RONALD ACUÑA JR.

BASEBALL'S SPEEDY SLUGGER

by Matt Chandler

CAPSTONE PRESS
a capstone imprint

Published by Capstone Press, an imprint of Capstone
1710 Roe Crest Drive, North Mankato, Minnesota 56003
capstonepub.com

Copyright © 2026 by Capstone. All rights reserved. No part of this publication may be reproduced in whole or in part, or stored in a retrieval system, or transmitted in any form or by any means, electronic, mechanical, photocopying, recording, or otherwise, without written permission of the publisher.

SPORTS ILLUSTRATED KIDS is a trademark of ABG-SI LLC. Used with permission.

Library of Congress Cataloging-in-Publication Data
Names: Chandler, Matt author
Title: Ronald Acuña Jr : baseball's speedy slugger / by Matt Chandler.
Description: North Mankato, Minnesota : Capstone Press, 2026. | Series: Sports illustrated kids stars of sports | Includes bibliographical references and index. | Audience term: juvenile | Audience: Ages 8-11 Capstone Press | Audience: Grades 4-6 Capstone Press | Summary: "In 2018, Ronald Acuña Jr. made his MLB debut. He was the youngest player in the league. He had multiple setbacks that season, but he still won the National League Rookie of the Year award. With his speed, explosive hitting ability, and incredible defense in the outfield, Acuña has continued to set records and win awards every season. From his childhood in Venezuela to his rise to baseball stardom, learn all about Acuña's life and career. This biography showcases how dedication and hard work can make dreams come true"— Provided by publisher.
Identifiers: LCCN 2024054599 (print) | LCCN 2024054600 (ebook) | ISBN 9798875222818 (hardcover) | ISBN 9798875222764 (paperback) | ISBN 9798875222771 (pdf) | ISBN 9798875222788 (epub) | ISBN 9798875222795 kindle edition)
Subjects: LCSH: Acuña, Ronald, Jr., 1997-—Juvenile literature. | Baseball players—United States—Biography—Juvenile literature. | Baseball players—Venezuela—Biography—Juvenile literature. | LCGFT: Biographies
Classification: LCC GV865.A264 C43 2026 (print) | LCC GV865.A264 (ebook) | DDC 796.357092 [B]—dc23/eng/20250212
LC record available at https://lccn.loc.gov/2024054599
LC ebook record available at https://lccn.loc.gov/2024054600

Editorial Credits
Editor: Patrick Donnelly; Designer: Sarah Bennett; Media Researcher: Svetlana Zhurkin; Production Specialist: Tori Abraham

Image Credits
Associated Press: File/Atlanta Journal-Constitution/Miguel Martinez, 5, Four Seam Images/Mike Janes, 9, 11, 13; Getty Images: Adam Glanzman, 18, 27, Andy Lyons, 17, Atlanta Braves/Matthew Grimes Jr., 24, Clarkson Creative/Tyler Schank, 26, Joe Sargent, cover, Kevin C. Cox, 19, 23, 28, Todd Kirkland, 20, Tom Szczerbowski, 7; Newscom: Icon Sportswire/Mark LoMoglio, 15, Icon Sportswire/Russell Lansford, 21; Shutterstock: Eugene Onischenko, 1

Source Notes
Page 6, "I lived for baseball . . ." Ronald Acuña Jr., "I mean no harm, I swear," The Players' Tribune, March 27, 2024, https://projects.theplayerstribune.com/ronald-acuna-jr-atlanta-braves-mlb-baseball/p/1. Accessed November 2024.

Page 7, "Ever since I was young . . ." Terence Moore, "Ronald Acuña Jr. takes flight," Atlanta Magazine, March 29, 2024, https://www.atlantamagazine.com/great-reads/ronald-acuna-jr-takes-flight/. Accessed November 2024.

Page 9, "Keep working hard . . ." Ronald Acuña Jr., "I mean no harm, I swear," The Players' Tribune, March 27, 2024, https://projects.theplayerstribune.com/ronald-acuna-jr-atlanta-braves-mlb-baseball/p/1. Accessed November 2024.

Page 10, "I was just so sad . . ." Ronald Acuña Jr., "I mean no harm, I swear," The Players' Tribune, March 27, 2024, https://projects.theplayerstribune.com/ronald-acuna-jr-atlanta-braves-mlb-baseball/p/1. Accessed November 2024.

Page 16, "Pack up your things . . ." Ronald Acuña Jr., "I mean no harm, I swear," The Players' Tribune, March 27, 2024, https://projects.theplayerstribune.com/ronald-acuna-jr-atlanta-braves-mlb-baseball/p/1. Accessed November 2024.

Any additional websites and resources referenced in this book are not maintained, authorized, or sponsored by Capstone. All product and company names are trademarks™ or registered® trademarks of their respective holders.

Printed and bound in China. 006276

TABLE OF CONTENTS

RECORD SETTER **4**

CHAPTER ONE
TEENAGE TALENT **6**

CHAPTER TWO
MINOR-LEAGUE STAR **10**

CHAPTER THREE
ROOKIE ON THE RISE **16**

CHAPTER FOUR
SPEED AND POWER **22**

CHAPTER FIVE
MVP **26**

TIMELINE. 29
GLOSSARY. 30
READ MORE. 31
INTERNET SITES 31
INDEX 32

Words in **BOLD** are in the glossary.

RECORD SETTER

On September 27, 2023, the Atlanta Braves faced the Chicago Cubs. A win would give the Braves home field advantage in the playoffs. But Atlanta trailed 5–4 in the bottom of the 10th inning. Ronald Acuña Jr. stepped to the plate with a runner on second base. The speedy star ripped a line drive to right field for a single to tie the game.

But Acuña didn't settle for just tying the game. On the next pitch, he broke for second base. Acuña easily beat the throw for his 70th stolen base of the season! He became the first player in Major League Baseball (MLB) history to hit 40 home runs and steal 70 bases in the same season.

For a moment, the game stopped. The crowd cheered as Acuña picked up second base and held it high over his head. Then, he finished off his record-setting night the best way possible. He scored the winning run.

>>> Ronald Acuña Jr. celebrates his 70th stolen base of the 2023 season.

CHAPTER ONE
TEENAGE TALENT

La Sabana, Venezuela, had only one baseball field when Ronald Acuña Jr. was growing up. He and his friends played ball every day after school. His dream, from as early as he can remember, was to be a professional baseball player.

"I lived for baseball," he once said. "Me and my friends, we played the game everywhere—down at the beach, on the huge lot behind the town hospital, out on the street. It was all we wanted to do."

Acuña had a large family. As a minor-league player, his dad traveled a lot for baseball. His mom and grandmother became two of his biggest cheerleaders. Acuña is the oldest of four brothers. He loved the game. But he also saw baseball as a way to support his family and make everyone's dreams come true.

》》》 Former Royals shortstop Alcides Escobar is Acuña's cousin.

"Ever since I was young, I had no choice but to become a superstar," he told a reporter in 2024. "I had to outcompete everyone."

Family Tree

Acuña comes from a baseball family. His cousin Kelvim Escobar won 101 games as a major-league pitcher. Another cousin, Alcides Escobar, won a World Series with the Kansas City Royals. His dad, Ronald Sr., played in the minor leagues. And his grandfather, Romualdo Blanco, pitched in the minors for six seasons.

CHASING A DREAM

Venezuela has produced many incredible professional baseball players through the years. Major-League **scouts** often visit the South American country to discover the next future stars. By the time he was 15, Acuña was already drawing the attention of MLB scouts. He attended many tryouts, showing off his speed, power, and strong defense. But no matter how many tryouts he went to, no scouts signed him to a contract. Giving up would have been easy. Instead, Acuña said the challenge made him work even harder. That hard work paid off.

In 2014, when he was 16 years old, a scout for the Atlanta Braves called. He wanted Acuña to sign his first professional baseball contract. The Braves gave him a $100,000 signing bonus. His mom offered something even more valuable: advice.

⟩⟩⟩ Acuña during a minor-league game in 2015

"Keep working hard," Acuña recalled his mom telling him before he left to join his minor-league teammates. "We want to go see you in the major leagues. So keep working."

CHAPTER TWO
MINOR-LEAGUE STAR

Acuña began his minor-league career more than 1,500 miles (2,400 kilometers) from home in North Port, Florida. The teen was assigned to the Gulf Coast League Braves. Acuña played in 55 games during his first season in the minor leagues. He had a .269 batting average and stole 16 bases. But off the field, Acuña struggled with being so far from home.

"I was just so sad. Missing everyone," he recalled. "That feeling lasted for about three or four months. Every time I was alone somewhere and thought of my parents, or I saw them in a photo, tears would fall."

FACT

Acuña spoke only Spanish when he arrived in the United States. He has said one of the biggest **cultural** challenges was trying to order food at restaurants.

Acuña moved through four levels of the minor leagues in his first two seasons. He was getting closer to the major leagues with every step. As he settled into life in the United States, Acuña began to show the talent that the scout had seen back in Venezuela. The teenager put up solid numbers. He stole 30 bases in his first two seasons and hit close to .300.

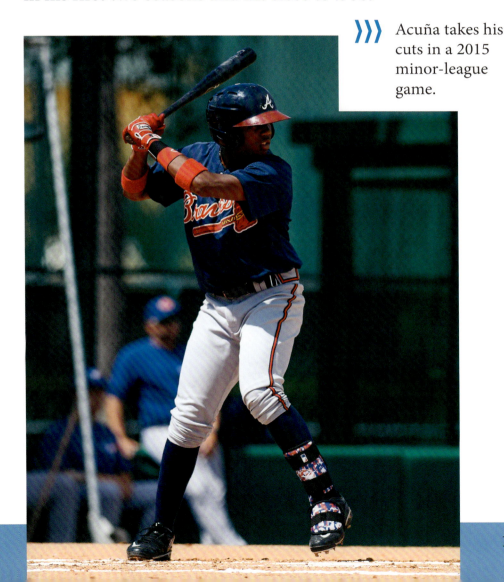

》》》 Acuña takes his cuts in a 2015 minor-league game.

11

BREAKOUT SEASON

By 2017, Acuña was showing the talent that earned him that big signing bonus. The Braves quickly **promoted** him. By midseason, Acuña had been moved to the Braves' top minor-league team, the Gwinnett Braves. The 19-year-old was one step away from his dream of playing in the majors.

In his Gwinnett debut, Acuña showed off his power. Facing future big-leaguer Tyler Danish, Acuña got a pitch he liked. He smashed the ball to right field. It cleared the fence for a home run.

Acuña finished the 2017 season hitting .325 with 21 home runs, 82 runs batted in (RBIs), and 88 runs scored. He added 44 stolen bases. Acuña was ready for the big leagues.

FACT

Acuña was named *USA Today*'s Minor League Player of the Year in 2017.

>>> Acuña shows his speed in a 2017 Gwinnett Braves game.

13

READY FOR THE SHOW

In 2018, the Braves invited Acuña to take part in spring training. He had a chance to earn a spot on the Braves opening day roster. Acuña responded by having an incredible spring. In 16 games he hit .432 with four home runs and four stolen bases.

Acuña's biggest game of the spring came against the New York Yankees. He stepped to the plate in the first inning and drilled a fastball to deep center field. It sailed into the stands for a home run! Acuña finished the day with three hits, two RBIs, and a run scored.

Many believed the rookie was a lock to make the big-league roster. But, in a move that surprised many people, the Braves sent Acuña back to the minors to start the regular season. However, his wait wouldn't be long.

>>> Acuña launches a home run in a 2018 spring training game.

CHAPTER THREE
ROOKIE ON THE RISE

On April 24, 2018, Acuña was in his hotel room resting before another night of minor-league baseball. The season had barely started. Then there was a knock on the door. It was his manager.

"Pack up your things now," he told Acuña. "You're going to the major leagues."

The next day, Acuña was in the visitor's locker room in Cincinnati. His locker held an Atlanta Braves jersey with his name on the back. His dream had come true.

In his first big-league at bat, Acuña almost made magic. He turned on a fastball and gave it a ride. But a Cincinnati Reds outfielder caught the ball just short of the wall in the deepest part of the ballpark.

Then, in the eighth inning, the rookie slapped a ground ball up the middle. He raced to first base. He had his first big-league hit.

》》》 Acuña takes the field for his major-league debut on April 25, 2018.

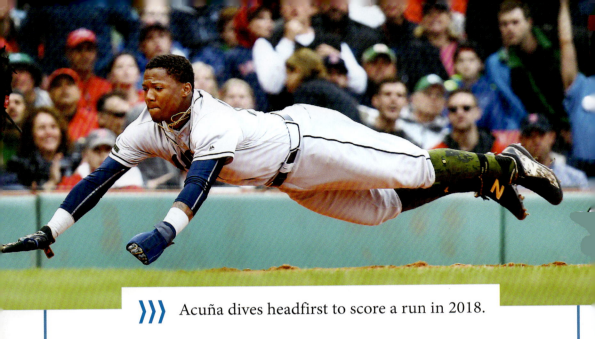

››› Acuña dives headfirst to score a run in 2018.

ROOKIE OF THE YEAR

For many players, adjusting to life in the big leagues can be hard. The competition is tougher. The season is longer. And for a top **prospect**, the attention can be overwhelming. Not for Acuña. The rookie lived up to the hype, showing off everything that made him a top prospect. He hit for power, showed off his speed, hit for a solid average, and played strong defense.

On a hot August night in Atlanta, Acuña led off the game against the Miami Marlins. He jumped on the first pitch and hammered a ball to deep left field for a home run. The blast set a record as Acuña became the youngest player to hit a home run in five consecutive games.

Acuña finished his rookie season with 26 home runs and 64 RBIs. He added 16 stolen bases. His play was impressive enough to earn him the National League (NL) Rookie of the Year Award. He beat out Washington Nationals rookie Juan Soto.

》》》 Acuña flexes his power swing with a home run against the Marlins in 2018.

FACT

In the 2018 NL Divisional Series, Acuña became the youngest player to hit a grand slam in the postseason.

ALL-STAR OUTFIELDER

Braves fans had high hopes for Acuña entering his first full season in the big leagues in 2019. He did not disappoint. Acuña's speed and power were on display all season. He drilled 41 home runs to lead the Braves. His 37 stolen bases were best in the NL. He also earned his first trip to the All-Star Game.

Over the next two seasons, Acuña showed flashes of brilliance. He also missed a lot of games because of injuries. When he was on the field, he continued to hit for power. And he showed off his excellent defense in the Braves outfield.

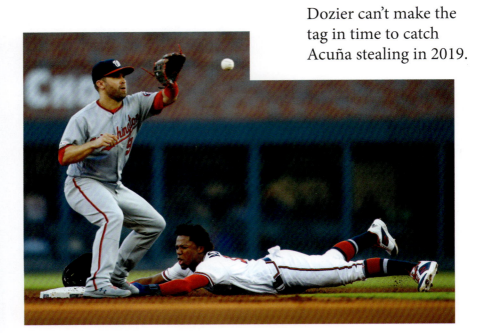

》》》 Washington Nationals second baseman Brian Dozier can't make the tag in time to catch Acuña stealing in 2019.

▶▶▶ Acuña follows through on a home run swing.

The 2020 season was shortened by the COVID-19 **pandemic**. Still, the Braves returned to the playoffs and reached the NL Championship Series. They faced the Los Angeles Dodgers. Each team had won three games. The winner of Game 7 would advance to the World Series. Acuña struggled. He went hitless on the night as the Braves lost 4–3. In the series, Acuña hit just .167 with no homers and only one stolen base. It was a heartbreaking way to end another great season.

Record-Setting Contract

On April 2, 2019, Acuña made history. The 21-year-old became the youngest player in MLB history to sign a contract worth at least $100 million. Acuña had been in the big leagues for less than one year, but the Braves saw a superstar in the making. His eight-year, $100 million deal guaranteed the Braves would keep their speedy outfielder in Atlanta through the 2026 season.

CHAPTER FOUR
SPEED AND POWER

In baseball, players are often seen as either hitting for power or having speed. It is rare for a player to do both. Acuña is arguably one of the fastest power hitters in the game. In more than 140 MLB seasons, only one player has hit 40 home runs and stolen 70 bases in a season. That's Acuña. His 73 stolen bases in 2023 set the Braves' modern-day record. Acuña led the NL in stolen bases twice in his first five seasons.

But his speed isn't limited to the basepaths. Acuña uses his speed in the outfield to chase down balls most players can't reach. He climbs outfield fences to take away home runs. He races into the gaps to cut off hits, keeping singles from turning into doubles.

Just ask Bryce Harper. In 2020, the Philadelphia Phillies slugger crushed a ball to the gap in right-center field. Acuña sprinted across the outfield at full speed. He made a diving catch to save at least a run and rob Harper of an extra-base hit.

》》》 Acuña leaps to steal a home run in 2023.

>>> Acuña drives the ball for a home run in 2023.

POWER THREAT

Acuña has plenty of power to go along with his blazing speed. In many games, he shows off both of his elite skills.

On September 19, 2023, the Braves were hosting the Phillies. Acuña crushed the first pitch he saw and sent it flying deep into the left field seats for a home run. In his third at bat, Acuña lined a single to left and immediately stole second base, his 67th steal of the season.

He wasn't done. One at bat later, Acuña swung at a fastball low in the strike zone and bombed his second home run of the night to dead center field. Thanks to his speed and power, the Braves beat the Phillies 9–3.

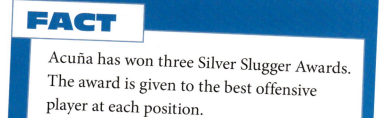

FACT

Acuña has won three Silver Slugger Awards. The award is given to the best offensive player at each position.

CHAPTER FIVE
MVP

On August 28, 2023, the Braves visited the Colorado Rockies. Acuña was in the middle of an amazing season. Fans were **debating** whether he or Los Angeles Dodgers superstar Mookie Betts would be the NL MVP. For many voters, Acuña answered that question with a single game.

He got started in the fifth inning with a long two-run homer to break a 2–2 tie. He added two singles and a double later in the game. Acuña scored four runs, drove in five, and stole a base. The Braves crushed the Rockies 14–4.

》》 Acuña celebrates after hitting a double in 2023.

Acuña finished the regular season with eye-popping numbers. In addition to a .337 batting average with 41 home runs, he had 217 hits, scored 149 runs, and stole 73 bases. The Braves won the NL East title. Acuña was rewarded for his huge offensive season by being the **unanimous** selection as NL MVP.

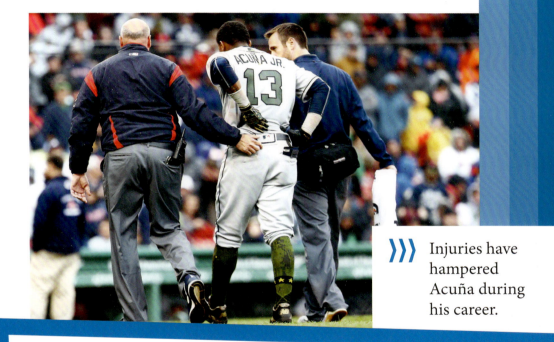

⟩⟩⟩ Injuries have hampered Acuña during his career.

Injury Bug

One setback for Acuña has been his inability to stay healthy. He has only played two full seasons since joining the Braves in 2018. He missed 80 games in 2021 after tearing the **ACL** in his right knee. He missed 113 games in 2024 after tearing the ACL in his left knee. Injuries to his hamstring, wrist, and back have also cost him playing time.

27

⟫ Acuña waits to take the field in 2024.

LOOKING TO THE FUTURE

Ronald Acuña Jr. is one of the most exciting players in the game. He hits for power, drives in runs, and has blazing speed. But he has also suffered serious injuries to each of his legs. Will he stay healthy enough to build a Hall of Fame career? Or will his injuries slow him down and hurt his success on the field? Time will tell. One thing is for certain: when he is healthy, Acuña is one of the most electrifying players in baseball.

TIMELINE

1998 — Ronald Jose Acuña Blanco Jr. is born in La Guaira, Venezuela, on December 18.

2014 — Acuña signs his first professional contract with the Atlanta Braves. He receives a $100,000 signing bonus.

2015 — Acuña makes his professional debut with the Gulf Coast Braves in the Rookie League.

2018 — On April 25, Acuña makes his major-league debut and picks up his first major-league hit with a single.

2018 — Acuña is named NL Rookie of the Year after finishing the season with 26 home runs, 64 RBIs, and 16 stolen bases.

2019 — Acuña becomes the youngest player in MLB history to sign a contract worth $100 million.

2021 — On July 10, Acuña tears the ACL in his right knee, sidelining him for the rest of the season.

2021 — With Acuña out of the lineup, the Braves win the World Series in six games over the Houston Astros.

2023 — Acuña wins the NL MVP Award.

2024 — On May 26, Acuña suffers the second serious injury of his career, tearing his left ACL. He misses the remainder of the season.

GLOSSARY

ACL (AY-SEE-ELL)—short for the anterior cruciate ligament, which helps stabilize the knee

CULTURAL (KUHL-chur-uhl)—relating to the ideas, customs, and social behavior of a society

DEBATE (duh-BAYT)—to argue many sides of a topic

PANDEMIC (pan-DEHM-ik)—a large outbreak of a transmittable disease

PROMOTE (pruh-MOWT)—to move to a higher rank or level of play

PROSPECT (PRAWSS-pekt)—a young player with high expectations of success

SCOUT (SKOWT)—a person whose job is to identify talent

UNANIMOUS (yew-NAN-uh-muhs)—with all in agreement

READ MORE

Berglund, Bruce. *Baseball GOATs: The Greatest Athletes of All Time.* North Mankato, MN: Capstone, 2022.

Calcaterra, Craig. *Legends of Major League Baseball.* New York: Abbeville Kids, 2023.

Chandler, Matt. *Baseball's Origin Story.* North Mankato, MN: Capstone, 2025.

INTERNET SITES

Atlanta Braves
mlb.com/braves

National Baseball Hall of Fame
baseballhall.org

Sports Illustrated: Ronald Acuña
si.com/mlb/player/ronald-Acuña-jr

INDEX

ACL, 27, 29, 30
Atlanta Braves, 4, 8, 10, 12, 13, 14, 16, 20, 21, 22, 25, 26, 27, 29

COVID-19, 21

Escobar, Alcides, 7

Gwinnett Braves, 12, 13

Major League Baseball, 2, 4, 8, 21, 22, 29
minor leagues, 6, 7, 9, 10, 11, 12, 16
Most Valuable Player (MVP) 26, 27, 29

National League, 19, 20, 21, 22, 26, 27, 29
New York Yankees, 14
NL Championship Series, 21

playoffs, 4, 21

Rookie of the Year Award, 19

Venezuela, 6, 8, 11, 29

Washington Nationals, 19, 20
World Series, 7, 21, 29

AUTHOR BIO

Matt Chandler is the author of more than 60 books for children and thousands of articles published in newspapers and magazines. He writes mostly nonfiction books with a focus on sports, ghosts and haunted places, and graphic novels. Matt lives in New York.